MY STATE! ★

Rhode Island

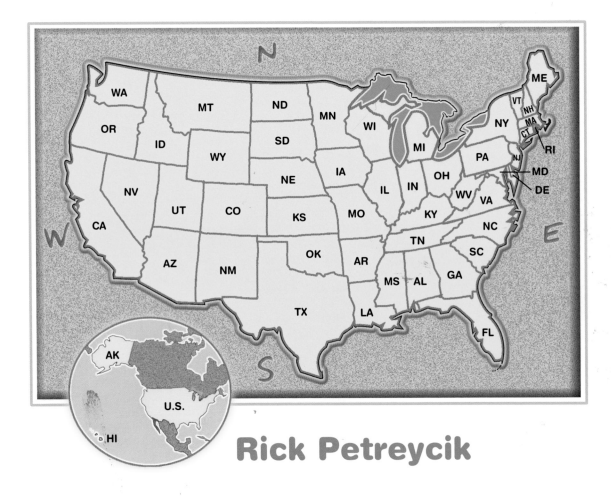

Rick Petreycik

mc Marshall Cavendish
Benchmark
New York

To my high school English teacher, Jay Reidy, for sparking my interest in writing, and to my wife, Pattilee, for her support and encouragement.

Series Consultant

David G. Vanderstel, Ph.D., Executive Director National Council on Public History

Marshall Cavendish Benchmark
99 White Plains Road
Tarrytown, New York 10591-9001
www.marshallcavendish.us

Maps, text, and illustrations copyright © 2005 by Marshall Cavendish Corporation
Maps and illustrations by Christopher Santoro

Library of Congress Cataloging-in-Publication Data

Petreycik, Rick.
Rhode Island / by Rick Petreycik.
p. cm. — (It's my state!)
Summary: "Surveys the history, government, and economy of Rhode Island, as
well as the diverse ways of life of its people"—Provided by publisher.
Includes bibliographical references and index.
ISBN 0-7614-1859-8 (alk. paper)
1. Rhode Island—Juvenile literature. I. Title. II. Series.

F79.3.P48 2005
974.5—dc22

2004030032

Back cover: The license plate shows Rhode Island's postal abbreviation followed by its year of statehood.
Photo research by Candlepants Incorporated
Cover photograph: Kindra Clineff /www.kindraclineff.com

The photographs in this book are used by permission and through the courtesy of: *Kindra Clineff / www.kindraclineff.com:* 48, 56, 70 (middle), 74. *Corbis:* 22, 30, 42, 51, 55 (top), 71 (bottom); W. Cody, 4 (top); Hal Horwitz, 4 (bottom); David H. Wells, 8, 53; Pat O'Hara, 19 (bottom); Catherine Karnow, 9, 14, 13, 57; Jean Guichard, 11; Bob Krist, 12, 71 (middle); Bettmann, 27, 37, 45 (top), 45 (bottom), 54 (top), 54 (bottom), 55 (bottom); Medford Historical Society Collection, 40; Joseph Sohm / ChromoSohm, Inc., 44; Nik Wheeler, 52; Larry Lee Photography, 63; Bob Rowan, 64, 67, 70 (top), 70, (bottom), 72; Onne van der Wal, 69, 73; Owaki-Kulla, 71 (top). *Northwind Picture Archives:* 24, 25, 34, 39. *Nativestock Pictures:* 46, 50.
Index Stock: Steve Dunwell, 58; Henry Horenstein, 10. *Photo Researchers, Inc.:* Chris Bjornberg, 4 (middle); Andrew J. Martinez, 5 (bottom); Stephen J. Krasemann, 18 (top); Jim Zipp, 18 (bottom); Michael P. Gadomski, 19 (middle), 16. *Marshall Cavendish:* KA, 5 (top), 5 (middle). *Super Stock:* David Forbert, 66. *The Image Works:* Peter Hvizdak, 17. *AnimalsAnimals / Earth Scenes:* Harry Engels, 18 (middle). *Bill Lindner Photography:* 19 (top). *Minden Pictures:* Tom Vezo, 21. *Art Resource, NY:* National Portrait Gallery, Smithsonian Institution, 54 (middle). *All Rights Reserved the Historical Society of Rhode Island:* Sarah Helen Whitman/Albumen Print/Coleman Remington Photographic Studio/RHi(x3)3055, 55 (middle).

Series design by Anahid Hamparian

Printed in Italy
1 3 5 6 4 2

Contents

A Quick Look at Rhode Island 4

1 The Ocean State 7
Plants & Animals 18

2 From the Beginning 23
Making a Pomander Ball 32
Important Dates 45

3 The People 47
Recipe for Johnny Cakes 51
Famous Rhode Islanders 54
Calendar of Events 56

4 How It Works 59
Branches of Government 60

5 Making a Living 65
Products & Resources 70

State Flag and Seal 75
Rhode Island Map 76
State Song 77
More About Rhode Island 78
Index 79

A Quick Look at Rhode Island

Tree: **Red Maple**

The red maple is widespread in Rhode Island and is easily recognized by its brilliant cluster of orange and red flowers, which appear in early spring. The flowers then turn into reddish-colored leaves that eventually turn green.

Bird: **Rhode Island Red**

The Rhode Island Red is well-known for the quality of its meat and eggs. This special breed of hen was introduced on a farm in the town of Little Compton in the 1850s. It was chosen as Rhode Island's state bird in 1954.

Flower: **Violet**

In 1968, the violet (scientific name, Viola sororia) was made the state flower. These violets have striking deep purple or blue petals. Violets can be found in Rhode Islanders' gardens, or growing wild in the state's fields and forests.

Mineral: Bowenite

Bowenite is named after George Bowen, a Rhode Island geologist (a scientist who studies earth structures, such as minerals and rocks) who discovered it in the 1800s. This mineral is found mainly in northern sections of Rhode Island and can be different colors ranging from yellow to gray to brown. Bowenite was made the state mineral in 1966.

Rock: Cumberlandite

Scientists estimate that Cumberlandite rocks are a little more than one billion years old. The rocks are usually dark brown or black, with white and gray markings. The state rock can be found around Narragansett Bay. The state made Cumberlandite its official rock in 1966.

State Shell: Quahog

In 1987, Rhode Island named the quahog its official state shell. The quahog is a thick-shelled, edible clam that can be found along Narragansett Bay. Native Americans in the region used the quahog shells to make wampum beads which were then used for such things as jewelry, decorative pieces, and for trade.

RHODE ISLAND

Wallum Lake

Pascoag

Chepachet River

BLACKSTONE RIVER

Woonsocket

Chepachet

Pawtucket

Jerimoth Hill

Providence

Scituate Reservoir

Foster

Cranston

Pawtuxet River

PROVIDENCE RIVER

West Warwick

Warwick

MOUNT HOPE BAY

Flat River Reservoir

Tiverton

WOOD RIVER

NARRAGANSETT BAY

SAKONNET RIVER

Portsmouth

Newport

Ashaway

INDIAN CEDAR SWAMP

GREAT SWAMP

Worden Pond

Point Judith Pond

Fort Adams State Park

Charlestown

Royal Indian Burial Ground

RHODE ISLAND SOUND

N

W

E

BLOCK ISLAND SOUND

S

Block Island National Wildlife Refuge

ATLANTIC OCEAN

BLOCK ISLAND

1 The Ocean State

There is an old saying about good things coming in small packages. One can definitely say that about Rhode Island, the United States' smallest state. The state spans only 1,214 square miles. The distance from Rhode Island's northern border to its southern border is 48 miles, while its distance from east to west is only 37 miles. Assuming there are no traffic problems on the roads, a person can drive across the entire state in less than an hour. But despite its size, Rhode Island has plenty to offer.

Water plays a big part in Rhode Island's geography. The state is bordered by sounds, bays, inlets, and the Atlantic Ocean. If a person added together the rough and jagged coastline along Narragansett Bay, plus the shorelines of Rhode Island's more than thirty islands, the state has a stunning total coastline of 384 miles.

Most of the state's natural features are a result of glacial

Rhode Island's Borders
North: Massachusetts
South: Block Island Sound, Rhode Island Sound, and the Atlantic Ocean
East: Massachusetts
West: Connecticut

Narragansett Bay is a popular place for both residents and tourist.

movement. Tens of thousands of years ago, a huge glacier—a slow-flowing body of ice—moved south from the land we now know as Canada and covered the region that includes Rhode Island and much of the northeastern part of the United States. As it moved, it cut into the solid rock that lay beneath the earth's loose surface material. It also helped shape hills, carrying sand, clay, and rocks in the process. With time, the glacier began to melt and move back toward the north. The melting ice formed rivers. Water from the rushing rivers then washed gravel, sand, and other material onto the surrounding plains. It pushed up rocky cliffs and carved out lakes and ponds. The rushing water also created channels leading to the ocean.

Changes in the land over millions of years have formed land features such as this lake.

Natural changes to the land are responsible for many of Rhode Island's inland bodies of water. But some of the state's water bodies were man-made. Whether they were formed by natural forces or by human ingenuity, there are more than three hundred reservoirs, ponds, and freshwater lakes found in Rhode Island.

Scituate Reservoir is the state's largest reservoir. In the 1920s, a dam was built on a section of the Pawtuxet River, creating the main Scituate Reservoir. This reservoir provides water to most of the state.

Many people like to live near the beaches. During storms, however, their homes can suffer a lot of damage.

The Coastal Lowlands

Rhode Island is made up of two major regions: the Coastal Lowlands and the Eastern New England Upland. The Coastal Lowlands cover more than half of Rhode Island. These lowlands include the eastern section of the state, all of its islands, and a strip of land east of Narragansett Bay. The Coastal Lowlands region is mostly made up of sandy beaches, saltwater ponds, marshes, and lagoons. The many beaches along this area are constantly changing. This is because waves and currents from the Atlantic Ocean move the sand from one area and deposit it into another. When weather conditions are stormy, the sand is swept back into the ocean.

One of the state's most well-known islands is also Rhode Island's southernmost point. Block Island is located in Block Island Sound, about 12 miles from the Rhode Island coast. The island—which is only 7 miles long and 3 miles wide—is not connected to the mainland by any bridges or tunnels. The only way to get there is by plane or boat. Block Island is home to

This lighthouse can be found on Block Island. Lighthouses on the coasts and islands help to guide ships in the night and during storms.

nature trails, historic buildings, lighthouses, resorts, and other relaxing tourist attractions. But it is also the home of about 800 year-round residents and functions much like many other towns in the state. The residents of the island have their own town government, school system, and other public services.

Narragansett Bay is another one of Rhode Island's well-known natural features. The shores of the bay are marked by rocky cliffs. Narragansett Bay is connected to other smaller bays, such as Greenwich Bay and Mount Hope Bay, and to many rivers including the Providence River.

In and around Narragansett Bay are several islands. Each of these islands is populated by towns and cities. The island named Rhode Island is also referred to as Aquidneck Island and is home

The cliff walk in Newport is a popular region. You can enjoy the view of the coast as well as the historic mansions.

to cities that include Newport, Portsmouth, and Middletown. Newport is one of Rhode Island's most famous cities. It has played an important role in the state's history and is a favorite site for visitors to Rhode Island.

As you head east of the bay, the hills are softly rounded and wooded. To the west of the bay, one may notice that the surrounding area has more forests and trees. Farther west, into the mainland—the main part of Rhode Island that is connected to Massachusetts and Connecticut—the ground gradually increases in elevation.

Many people have made Rhode Island cities like Providence their home.

Providence, Rhode Island's capital, is located on the mainland near the Providence River. Other towns and cities on the mainland coastal lowlands include Warwick, Cranston, Woonsocket, Charlestown, and Westerly.

The Eastern New England Upland

The Eastern New England Upland, which extends from Connecticut to Maine, stretches through the northern and western regions of Rhode Island. It covers about a third of the state's total area. Rolling hills, narrow valleys, wooded areas, ponds, lakes, and reservoirs mark this scenic region, which is also called the Western Rocky Upland. As you travel across this region from east to west, the elevation gradually increases from about 200 feet to approximately 800 hundred feet. In the far western edge of the state—close to the Connecticut border—is Jerimoth Hill. At 812 feet above sea level, it is the highest point in Rhode Island.

The western portion of the state is dotted with small towns and cities, rivers, reservoirs, and lakes. Much of the land is ideal for growing crops such as hay, corn, and various fruits and vegetables.

Tree-filled forests can be found throughout the state.

The wooded areas in the region are filled with a variety of trees, including oak, maple, hickory, birch, pine, spruce, cedar and hemlock. Parts of Rhode Island's Upland are perfect for those who enjoy outdoor activities such as hiking, canoeing, fishing, and horseback riding.

Climate

Rhode Island's climate tends to be a lot milder than that of its other New England neighbors. This means that Rhode Island—mostly the southern, southeastern, and coastal areas—usually has warmer winter temperatures. The higher temperatures are a result of the winds blowing in from the Atlantic Ocean and Narragansett Bay. The northern and northwestern sections of Rhode Island tend to have cooler year-round temperatures than southern and coastal Rhode Island. In the summer, the coast and the southern portions of the state are slightly warmer than the northern sections.

In general, the coldest months in the state are January and February. During January, Rhode Islanders can expect an average temperature of about 29 degrees Fahrenheit. The lowest temperature occurred on February 5, 1996, when the city of Greene recorded a very chilly minus 25 degrees.

The warmest months in Rhode Island are July and August. The average temperature during that period is about 71 degrees. The heat became pretty intense for residents of Providence on August 2, 1975, when the temperature climbed to a record-breaking 104 degrees Fahrenheit.

Precipitation is the amount of water that falls as either rain, snow, or other moisture. Rhode Island's average precipitation is about 44 inches per year, though the southwestern part of the state tends to be wetter than the rest of Rhode Island. The Ocean State's yearly snowfall amounts to about 31 inches.

Hurricanes have been the most destructive weather events Rhode Islanders living in coastal areas have had to deal with over the years. They usually strike in late summer and early fall. The strong winds of the hurricane damage and destroy homes and other buildings. The heavy rains brought in by the hurricanes often cause flooding. Flooding and structural damage to buildings can also be caused by strong and tall waves brought in by the hurricane. Throughout Rhode Island's history, hurricanes have caused millions of dollars worth of damage.

In 1966, the U.S. Army Corps of Engineers built a hurricane barrier on part of the Providence River. This barrier is supposed to prevent flooding in downtown Providence during hurricanes and coastal storms.

Wild Life

Rhode Island plays host to a wide variety of plants and animals. More than 60 percent of Rhode Island is forested—or has wooded areas. Around sixty different species—or types—of trees thrive in Rhode Island. These include ashes,

A shagbark hickory tree.

hickories, elms, maples, poplars, beeches, willows, birches, sugar maples, and Atlantic white cedars. Inland fields are often dotted with colorful wildflowers, such as goldenrod, asters, violets, and lilies during the warm seasons. Flowering plants also populate the state's wooded areas, and among these are mountain laurels, wild roses, dogwoods, azaleas, blue gentians, orchids, irises, and rhododendrons.

Among the many wild mammals that roam Rhode Island's wooded areas are white-tailed deer, skunks, rabbits, raccoons, squirrels, moles, foxes, and woodchucks. Beavers, muskrats, otters, and minks can be spotted swimming in the state's many ponds, rivers, and lakes. Other inhabitants of these freshwater areas include fish such as bass, perch, pike, trout, and pickerel.

In the salty waters of the coasts you may find swordfish, striped bass, flounder, shark, tuna, mackerel, jellyfish, bluefish, cod, and butterfish. Shellfish also thrive in Rhode Island's coastal areas, particularly lobsters, soft-shell crabs, oysters, scallops, mussels, and clams.

Harbor seals can be found in coastal waters.

Plants & Animals

White-Tailed Deer

These swift, graceful animals have red-brown fur in the summer that changes to a grayish-brown during the winter months. An adult male deer—called a buck—can grow to weigh nearly 300 pounds. Young white-tailed deer—called fawns—have reddish-brown fur dotted with white spots to help camouflage the young animal. As the deer gets older, the spots disappear.

Muskrat

This large rodent can grow to be more than 14 inches long and is covered with brownish fur. Muskrats make their homes around Rhode Island's numerous ponds, lakes, and rivers by piecing together piles of twigs, branches, leaves, and other plant material. A muskrat's flattened tail—which acts like a boat's rudder—and its partially webbed back feet come in handy when the animal swims from one spot to another.

Blue Jay

This woodland bird, which is part of the crow family, is easily recognized by its bright blue, black, and white color, and the pointy crest at the top of its head. Blue jays may be as large as 12 inches, and eat mostly insects, nuts, and seeds.

Bluefish

Bluefish are a common sight along Rhode Island's Atlantic coastline, particularly in the spring when they prey on other fish moving toward the shore to breed. Catching bluefish and their young, known as snappers, is a popular sport in Rhode Island. The largest bluefish caught on record weighed in at slightly over 25 pounds. But bluefish usually weigh between 5 and 15 pounds.

Goldenrod

Goldenrod is a wildflower that graces Rhode Island's meadows, woods, and hills in autumn. It has a wand-like stem with clusters of brilliant yellow-colored flowers. The plant can grow to a height of 4 feet.

Paper Birch

Sometimes called white birches or canoe birches, paper birch trees are found mainly in Rhode Island's northern wooded areas. The trees have sheets of bark that peel off the tree in layers—which reminds people of paper. In the past, Native Americans used the sturdy but flexible bark of these tall trees to build canoes.

Rhode Island also has many birds, and more than 250 species of our flying friends have been spotted in the state. In Rhode Island's wooded areas you will see robins, owls, blue jays, flickers, sparrows, and catbirds. Looking for meals of fish and shellfish along the coast are seagulls, terns, osprey, and loons. Geese and ducks also make their homes near the state's waterways. Rhode Island also has some game birds which are often hunted during specific times of the year. Some of the game birds include pheasants, wild ducks, quails, and partridges.

Rhode Island has gone to great lengths to protect its wildlife. However, the increase in human habitation added to a rise in pollution over the years has put some of the state's wildlife at risk of disappearing completely. Animals that are already on the state's threatened or endangered species lists include the bald eagle, the piping plover, the American burying beetle, and other fish, amphibians, reptiles, and mammals.

Organizations like the Rhode Island Audubon Society and the Rhode Island Department of Environmental Management have been trying to prevent many of these animals and plants from disappearing. Working together with the state and federal government alongside concerned Rhode Islanders, these groups and organizations have managed to find ways to help protect Rhode Island's wildlife. The government has used some of the state's money to sponsor programs that protect habitats, support breeding programs, and other activities that inform the public about the need for preservation and conservation of land and wildlife. Laws and other legislation have also been passed to protect specific animals from being hunted, harmed, or from having their habitat disrupted or destroyed. Rhode Islanders are serious about protecting their beautiful land and the wildlife that inhabits it.

The piping plover population in Rhode Island is threatened. These small birds make their nests along the sandy beaches.

2 From the Beginning

Many historians and scientists estimate that the first human inhabitants of the region that now includes Rhode Island arrived around 12,000 B.C.E. These people were most likely the ancestors of present-day Native Americans. They were mainly hunters and gatherers who looked for food in the area's thick forests and sparkling coastal waters. These early residents lived in small communities and made tools out of stone. Eventually, they began growing crops such as corn, beans, squash, cucumbers, tobacco, and pumpkins.

Their Native American descendants remained in the area. Historians think that in the early seventeenth century—just before the first white settlers arrived in the region—there were about 10,000 Native Americans living in the area. The Natives were made up of five different groups: the Nipmuc, the Niantic, the Wampanoag, the Narragansett, and the Pequot. All of these people were a part of the Algonquian family, which was a large collection of northeastern Native American groups that shared the same language and customs. Most of the Native Americans living in the region that now includes Rhode Island settled in

Two boys pose for a picture in the early 1900s. Young children often had to work to help support their families.

23

A European artist's impression of a Wampanoag warrior.

villages close to bodies of water. This gave them easy access to sources of food and trade. Their homes were called wigwams, which were round-roofed structures with frames made of wooden poles. The frames were covered with deer hide, bark from trees, or reeds that were stitched together. Except for occasional battles between the Narragansett (the largest and most powerful group in the region) and the Wampanoag (who inhabited the far eastern parts), the Native Americans managed to live together peacefully. They also had a remarkable system of government in which village leaders who functioned as judges decided upon legal and spiritual disputes.

The First European Settlers

In the early 1500s, it was possible that Portuguese navigators spotted the land now known as Rhode Island as they sailed by. However the first European to actually explore the area was an Italian sailor named Giovanni da Verrazzano. Sailing for France in 1524, Verrazzano landed near present-day Block Island. He thought the land closely resembled the Mediterranean island of Rhodes, so he named the area Rhode Island.

In 1614 Adriaen Block, a Dutch navigator, was the next European to venture into Rhode Island's waters. Block Island is named after him. Fourteen years

Adriaen Block is shown with his crew building more ships on the Rhode Island coast.

later, a religious group from England known as the Puritans had started a colony north of Rhode Island. It was called the Massachusetts Bay Colony, and its main areas of settlement were Boston and Salem. They had left their native country because they disagreed with the Church of England. They believed in firm obedience to their own church laws, which were strictly enforced by the colony's governor, John Winthrop.

Some experts say that Rhode Island got its name from Adriaen Block instead of Verrazzano. When Block spoke about the land we now refer to as Aquidneck Island, he called it *Roodt Eylandt* because of the land's reddish-colored clay. (At that time, *Roodt* meant "red" and *Eylandt* meant "island.").

In 1628, a preacher named Roger Williams arrived in Boston. Unlike the other Puritans of Massachusetts Bay, Williams believed in complete religious freedom. He believed that each individual should be free to worship God in the manner he or she chooses. He also believed that the laws of church should be separate from the laws of government. These beliefs conflicted with the rules of the Massachusetts Bay Colony.

Because of his firm convictions and outspoken nature, the Puritan authorities considered Williams a dangerous threat and arrested him on several occasions. In 1636 his preaching on behalf of religious freedom had angered the Puritan officials so much that Governor Winthrop had planned to send him back to England.

Williams found out about the governor's plan, and quickly fled south, traveling across icy streams and thickly forested areas blanketed by heavy snow. Within a few days, he arrived at the eastern side of Narragansett Bay, where the

A European artist's idea of how Roger Williams met the Native Americans who helped him.

Wampanoag and their leader, Massasoit, welcomed him. He stayed with the Native Americans throughout the winter.

Soon other white settlers seeking religious freedom joined him. In June of 1636, Williams purchased some land from Massasoit and two other Narragansett Natives, Canonicus and Miantonomo. The land was located at the northern tip of Narragansett Bay. He named it Providence, because he felt that God's providence, or "watchful eye," had kept him safe from harm and guided him on his trip from Boston.

Word about Williams' new colony and its spirit of religious and political freedom began to spread throughout Massachusetts Bay, attracting even more settlers to Providence. In addition, other religious and political leaders seeking similar freedoms came to the area. They, in turn, established settlements in the area that now includes present-day Portsmouth, Newport, and Warwick.

In 1644 the English Parliament granted Williams a charter that recognized all four settlements as the colony of Providence Plantations. In 1647 representatives from each settlement met at Portsmouth. They set up a system of government that included a representative assembly and a president. It was decided that the settlements' male inhabitants would elect the president.

By the 1650s Roger Williams' vision of religious freedom and tolerance for all made Rhode Island a popular place for people who practiced different religions.

In 1663 the English king, Charles II, granted the four settlements a royal charter. This charter provided the new colony with a larger amount of self-government—more than any of the other English colonies in North America, including Connecticut, Massachusetts Bay, and Virginia. It also authorized the colony to continue Roger Williams's "lively experiment" of freedom of religion for all.

King Philip's War

For nearly forty years after Roger Williams founded Providence, Rhode Island's colonists had friendly relations with the area's Native Americans. That is partly because Williams believed that since the Native American people were the first inhabitants of the area and were therefore the rightful owners, they should be paid for land that the colonists wanted. In other colonies, however, settlers were taking land from local Native Americans without paying them. As a result, some of the Native American groups began to fight the colonists.

In 1675 a Wampanoag leader named Metacomet, whom the settlers called King Philip, began attacking English settlements. He also convinced other Native groups in the region—the Nipmuc, Mohegan, and Podunk—to join the Wampanoag in protecting Native lands. At first, King Philip only targeted colonial settlements in Massachusetts Bay. That changed, however, when militia—a group of trained fighters—from Connecticut and Massachusetts Bay attacked and defeated a group of Native American warriors in a southern Rhode Island town that is now called Kingston. The battle became known as the Great Swamp Fight.

But the colonial militia did not stop there. They continued to raid and burn surrounding Native American villages. Within a few days the colonists had killed more than a thousand Native American men, women, and children.

King Philip and Native American allies began attacking settlements in Rhode Island as well as Massachusetts Bay. They set Providence on fire, and settlers from the town and neighboring areas were forced to flee to the colony's many offshore islands. In 1676, King Philip was killed in a battle near present-day Bristol, Rhode Island. As a result of the war, which became known as King Philip's War, the Nipmuc, Mohegan, and Podunk groups were practically wiped out. Several hundred of King Philip's warriors were also captured and sold into slavery in other countries. The relationships between the Rhode Island colonists and the region's Native

Native Americans and colonists fought over land rights and other issues.

American people were never quite the same again. The ones who remained did not have much power against the white settlers. Some moved away, while others gave up their traditional lifestyles to fit in with the colonists.

Prosperity, Revolution, and Independence

The early 1700s marked the beginning of a period of great prosperity for Rhode Island. Farming and whaling were very profitable businesses. Sea trading was important to the colony's economy. In fact, the colony's merchants sold and traded everything from wood, salt, cider, dairy products, and molasses to horses, fish, and preserved meats. Rhode Island's coasts made it easy for ships to come in and sail out bearing goods and money. Within a short period of time, Newport and Providence had become two of the busiest ports in the world.

The most important link in making sure that Rhode Island's economy remained stable and profitable during this period was its trade relationship with the West Indies. (The West Indies are a group of islands in the Caribbean Sea.) Rhode Island's merchants found a way to strengthen that link by coming up with what came to be known as the Triangular Trade. Rhode Island merchants would send rum—a type of alcohol—to Africa. The rum had been made in Rhode Island using molasses from the West Indies. Once the rum arrived in Africa, it was exchanged for African slaves. The slaves—who were needed to work on the sugar plantations in the West Indies—were be shipped to the West Indies and traded for molasses. The molasses was then sent to Rhode Island and turned into additional rum. The cycle repeated over and over, bringing great profit to Rhode Island traders.

Making a Pomander Ball

Pomander balls were natural air fresheners commonly used in colonial homes for clearing out or masking odors. They were sometimes used in kitchens because of the smells from cooking in an open fireplace. These air fresheners are still popular today as holiday decorations or as gifts.

You will need:

Paper towels
A roll of masking tape (the tape should be about 1/4 inch wide)
A medium-sized orange
A nail or screw
20-30 whole cloves
1 tablespoon of ground cinnamon
1 tablespoon of ground nutmeg
1 tablespoon of ground allspice
Tissue paper (used for gifts)
3 feet of narrow ribbon (about 1/2 inch wide)

Spread some paper towel on your work surface. Wrap one piece of tape around the orange so that it divides it in half. Wrap another piece of tape around the orange, dividing into half the other way. (The tape should go around the orange as a ribbon would around a gift box.)

Use the nail or screw to make about twenty holes in the skin of the orange. Have an adult help you with this because nails and screws can be sharp. Poke holes all around the orange, but do not make holes through the tape.

Push the cloves into the orange, but do not put the cloves into the holes you just made. You can use the nail or screw to make new small holes for the cloves. Be sure not to put any cloves through the tape.

Remove the tape.

Mix the cinnamon, nutmeg, and allspice together on a piece of paper towel. Roll the orange around in the spices. You can push a some of the spices into the first holes you made with the nail.

Carefully wrap the orange in tissue paper. The orange needs to be stored in a cool, dark, and dry place for about three weeks. During this time it will shrink and become hard. Have an adult help you pick the right place—if the place where you store the orange is not dry and dark, the orange could get spoiled. Also make sure that any pets or animals cannot get to the orange.

When the orange is dried out, unwrap it and throw away the tissue paper. Wrap the ribbon around the orange, following the path you used for the masking tape. Have an adult help you if you need extra hands to tie the ribbon. Make a double knot at the top of the orange. Make a loop with the ends of the ribbon, and tie the loop with a bow. The loop can be used to hang the pomander ball.

Once it is ready, hang the ball to freshen a room or gift it as a great-smelling gift!

Around the same time that Rhode Island was experiencing its economic prosperity, England was involved in a struggle with France for control over most of North America. The struggle was known as the French and Indian War. England expected its colonies to contribute by providing troops and by paying taxes to help pay for the cost of the war. The fiercely independent Rhode Islanders felt differently. They said it was England's problem, not theirs.

But in 1764 the English Parliament dealt the colonists a heavy blow. It passed the Sugar Act, which charged a tax on goods imported into the colony, such as molasses, sugar, and wine. The taxes angered the colonists—especially the merchants who were involved in the triangular trade. The following year when Parliament passed the Stamp Act, which taxed all kinds of paper items—from legal documents to playing cards—the colonists were even more upset.

In protest and to get around the taxes imposed by the Sugar Act, some merchants began smuggling molasses, sugar, and other taxable goods into the colony. The colonists' general unrest eventually led to vio-lence. On June 10, 1772, a group of Providence mer-chants led by John Brown lured a British customs vessel named the *Gaspee* into the shallow waters of Narra-gansett Bay, boarded it, and

The burning of the Gaspee *by angry colonists.*

set it on fire. The ship's commander, Lieutenant William Dudington, was shot and wounded during the attack. This was the first time the New England colonists had actually taken up arms against the Crown.

When Massachusetts rose in rebellion against England less than three years later, Rhode Island immediately sent one thousand militiamen to help its colonial neighbor. It also put together a naval force. On May 4, 1776, Rhode Island became the first New England colony to reject allegiance to the Crown and declare independence—two months before the actual signing of the Declaration of Independence.

The Revolutionary War lasted from 1775 to 1783. During the war, many battles were fought throughout the colonies and Rhode Islanders participated in the fighting. Residents in the colony who supported independence also provided supplies, money, and food for the troops. No major battles were fought on Rhode Island soil, but the Battle of Rhode Island did occur within the colony's borders in 1778. This battle happened in Newport and involved the British, the Americans, and their French Allies. Serving with the American troops was a regiment of blacks. Part of the First Rhode Island Regiment, these soldiers were some for the first black troops to fight for the soon-to-be-independent country.

In 1783, the Revolutionary War came to a close. Rhode Island's feisty, independent spirit was still strongly evident. A constitution for the newly formed country was drafted to establish laws. Colonies were required to sign the Constitution in order to officially become part of the new country. But Rhode Island refused to ratify—or approve—the Constitution until the Bill of Rights was added. The Bill of Rights guarantees individual liberties such as freedom of religion. The other colonies finally agreed to the Bill of Rights, and on May 29, 1790, Rhode Island approved the Constitution and became the thirteenth state.

The Growth of Industries

In the late 1700s and into the 1800s, certain aspects of Rhode Island's economy began to prosper. A rich and powerful Providence merchant named Moses Brown had been operating a cotton-spinning mill in Pawtucket on the Blackstone River. He had visited Great Britain before and had witnessed how their cotton mills used water-powered machines to spin cotton into thread. These British mills were able to produce more products faster and at a lower cost. Brown wished he knew the secret to their operations, but British mill owners did not want competition from other countries, so they guarded their operations very carefully. In fact, anyone who worked in a water-powered cotton mill in England was forbidden to leave the country.

However, one mill worker did manage to slip out undetected. Samuel Slater disguised himself as a farmer, boarded a ship, and ended up in Pawtucket in 1790. He worked with Brown to create the same type of water-powered mill he had seen in England. The rolling Blackstone River was the perfect source for setting in motion a gigantic waterwheel. The waterwheel was attached to Brown's mill and created energy to power the mill's machinery. In 1793, Slater set up his own mill. Within a few years, other mills began to spring up along Rhode Island's many rivers. The textile industry in Rhode Island thrived.

The use of river currents and waterwheels to power mills was also applied to other industries. Following Slater's approach, David Wilkinson, another Pawtucket businessman, developed a water-powered mill that was used to manufacture metal tools and equipment.

As a result of the time- and labor-savings brought about by both Slater's and Wilkinson's inventions, many of Rhode Island's businesses shifted from farming, whaling, and sea trading to manufacturing and banking activities. People still practiced those other trades in the state, but they were not as prominent as in earlier years. In the 1840s through the 1850s, railroad lines began to cross through Rhode Island. These lines helped to connect Rhode Island to other states, making trade and business even more profitable.

Rhode Island's economy continued to grow. As word of the state's economic prosperity spread, it began to attract foreigners seeking better opportunities. As a steady stream of immigrants made their way into the state, Rhode Island's population skyrocketed from 69,122 in 1800 to 147,545 in 1850.

A mill in Pawtucket

Nehemiah Dodge, a Providence silversmith, had been fascinated with metals. In 1794, after conducting a number of experiments, he had perfected a way to make cheap metals look nicer. He found a way to cover the cheaper metals with better-looking and more expensive metals. Thanks to his discovery, Rhode Island entered the jewelry industry. By 1824, Providence had become the jewelry making capital of North America.

Sadly, however, these newcomers found they had little voice in the state's government. According to the royal charter that King Charles II had granted Rhode Island's colonists in 1663—and which was still in effect in the early nineteenth century—only male property owners and their oldest sons could vote. That meant that in 1840 only about 40 percent of the state's entire population could participate in the state government. The majority of that 40 percent lived in the state's rural areas, leaving those who worked in the crowded cities—including the newly arrived immigrants who could not afford to buy land—underrepresented in decisions about the state government.

In 1841 a Providence attorney named Thomas Dorr felt something had to be done. He started a reform movement to change the state's outdated charter. He formed the People's Party, and he and his followers held a People's Convention, which ratified a new constitution that extended voting rights to all males who lived within the state. Members of the party then held their own statewide election, and elected Dorr as their governor. Dorr was arrested, convicted of treason, and was

Over the years Providence became a busy city with many residents.

sentenced to life in prison. He was then released after serving only a year. Dorr's Rebellion—as his series of actions was called—led to a revised state constitution in 1843, which said that property ownership was no longer required in order for adult males to vote.

The Civil War

Differences in opinion between the northern states and the southern states started to cause problems. Issues having to do with slavery, agriculture, the economy, and government control were causing a division within the nation. Rhode Island imported a lot of cotton from the southern states to keep its textile mills running. So the state tended to sympathize with the South's concerns. In the late 1800s, when it appeared that war between North and South was coming, Rhode Island sent a group of delegates to a convention in Virginia to try to come up with a peaceful resolution. But when it came to the issue of slavery, many Rhode Island citizens were not willing to compromise. In 1860, the state ended up siding with Abraham Lincoln in an effort to abolish slavery as well as preserve the country as a whole.

But the southern states separated from the rest of the country. These southern states joined together to form the Confederacy. The Confederacy battled the Union—as the northern states were known—in many bloody battles throughout the country. The Civil War lasted from 1861 to 1865. Rhode Island factories and farmers provided food and supplies for Union troops. More than 24,000 Rhode Islanders fought

for the Union army. In the end, the northern states won the war and the Confederate states eventually rejoined the Union.

In the period after the Civil War, Rhode Island's economy and population continued to grow. The state's textile mills produced thread, yarn, cotton shirts, and other materials. These were then shipped to

Civil War soldiers from Rhode Island pose for a picture. Though many in the state supported the South, the state remained part of the Union.

countries all over the world. Rhode Island's jewelry and metal products industries were also thriving.

In the late 1800s, wealthy New York-based families such as the Astors, the Vanderbilts, the Morgans, and the Belmonts chose Newport as their summer vacation spot. (Members of these families were famous industrialists, which means they were known for their important roles in industry growth.) In fact, they were so fond of the area that they built huge and expensive mansions there.

A popular tourist attraction is a seventy-room summer retreat known as the Breakers. New York tycoon Cornelius Vanderbilt built it in the 1890s, and it is Newport's largest and most expensive mansion. Thirty-three of the mansion's rooms were set aside for Vanderbilt's servants alone. The main rooms are filled with finely polished marble and alabaster, glistening crystal chandeliers, deep velvet-colored draperies and cushions, and gold-covered walls.

The Modern Age

In the 1900s more immigrants were drawn to Rhode Island's industrial success. Most of the immigrants came from Italy, Ireland, Great Britain, Portugal, Russia, and French Canada.

Although these newcomers were usually better off than they had been in the countries they came from, they still faced rather harsh conditions in America. Many immigrants had fewer rights than American residents living in Rhode Island. These immigrants were often treated badly and were forced to take the harder and more unpleasant jobs that others did not want.

Several boys wait for the factory to open. Until laws were passed in the early 1900s, men, women, and children often worked in very dangerous conditions.

The factories that provided goods and money for the state economy were not pleasant places to work. Both citizens and immigrants often worked long hours in the factories, with little or no heat in the winter and very little fresh air during the hot summer months. Some of the machinery was dangerous to use and people could become injured using them. In some instances, even young children had to work in factories and mills to help their families earn enough money to buy food and clothing, and pay the rent. In the early 1900s some reform was made to try to prevent millworkers from these dangerous conditions. But the average working family still had a very difficult time making a living.

Unfortunately, by the time World War I erupted in 1914, many of Rhode Island's industries were no longer as profitable. The state still managed to provide supplies and troops to the American war effort. But many of the state's textile companies had moved their mills to the southern states. The warmer climate was better for growing cotton. They also discovered that southern laborers were willing to work for lower wages.

Things grew worse for the Ocean State—and for the rest of the country—when the Great Depression struck in 1929. The stock market collapsed and as a result, many people lost all of their money and businesses closed down. Thousands of people were out of work, and Rhode Island's once-thriving textile business had practically disappeared. Some residents left Rhode Island to search for jobs in other states. The federal government established some programs to help people find jobs and feed their families, but it was a very difficult time.

With the United States' entry into World War II in 1941, the economy began to improve. American factories reopened and began manufacturing goods for the war

> While Rhode Island's men were overseas fulfilling their military obligations during World War II, the state's women went to work in the factories. Between 1941 and 1945, women played a major role in producing about 17,000 torpedoes at the Naval Torpedo Station located at Newport's Goat Island.

effort. Farm products were again needed to feed the troops. Rhode Island's factories made a huge contribution by producing ammunition, chemicals, machinery, electronics, and other war materials.

Once the war was over, though, and Rhode Island's factories stopped building war materials, the number of people without jobs became alarmingly high again. To replace Rhode Island's textile industry, efforts were made to attract other types of businesses to help reduce the state's unemployment rate and boost its economy.

It took some time, but over the next several decades the hard work eventually paid off. Companies specializing in electronic equipment, plastics, machinery, chemicals, health care products, and toys began moving into the state, providing jobs as well as stimulating the economy. The government also provided a number of new jobs, as did the state's rising tourist trade.

Through the end of the twentieth century, Rhode Island continued to grow. It had its ups and downs as certain industries thrived and other failed. But residents continued to work together to improve their businesses, cities, schools, and state services.

Today Rhode Island is doing well. Its many new businesses continue to provide a wealth of jobs not only to Rhode Islanders, but also to commuters from neighboring Massachusetts and Connecticut. The state has also become increasingly popular with tourists from around the world who are interested in its colorful history and its natural beauty.

The Providence skyline.

Important Dates

12,000 BCE   Ancestors of present-day Native Americans inhabit the region. By the early sixteenth century, these early Natives had a population of about 10,000.

1524   Giovanni da Verrazzano explores Narragansett Bay.

1614   1614 Adriaen Block, a Dutch navigator, lands on the island that is now known as Block Island.

1636   Roger Williams establishes a colony in Providence. It is the first settlement in Rhode Island.

1644   The English Parliament grants Roger Williams a charter that recognizes the four settlements of Providence, Portsmouth, Newport, and Warwick as the colony of Providence Plantations.

Roger Williams

1663   King Charles II of England grants Providence Plantations a new royal charter, which provides the colonists with an even greater degree of self-government and religious freedom.

1675   During King Philip's War, militia from Connecticut and Massachusetts Bay defeat Native American warriors in the Great Swamp Fight near present-day Kingston.

1772   A group of Providence merchants led by John Brown set fire to the British customs vessel the *Gaspee* in Narragansett Bay.

1776   Rhode Island becomes the first colony to declare independence from England.

1790   On May 29, Rhode Island becomes the thirteenth state. Moses Brown and Samuel Slater open the first water-powered cotton spinning mill in the United States.

1843   Rhode Island's state constitution is revised, expanding voting rights.

Severe flooding

1861-1865   The Civil War is fought. More than 24,000 Rhode Islanders serve in the Union military.

1938   A hurricane and tidal wave kill hundreds and cause millions in damage.

1969   A $71 million bridge connects Jamestown to Newport over the Narragansett Bay.

1990   Rhode Island celebrates its bicentennial, or two-hundredth anniversary of statehood.

2004   A memorial was established on the grounds of the Rhode Island State House to honor Rhode Islanders who lost their lives fighting the war against terror.

3   The People

Before the Europeans came, the land that now includes Rhode Island was inhabited by Native Americans. Many Europeans eventually came to the region looking for new land and religious freedom. Until the early 1800s, most of these new settlers made their living by farming, fishing, shipbuilding, or trading.

As newer technologies were developed, manufacturing became a more important part of the economy. Factories involved in manufacturing began to spring up quickly in Rhode Island's major cities. With the increase in factories came the need for more people to work in them. As word of that need spread—particularly overseas to other countries—Rhode Island

A large number of French-Canadians moved to the northern city of Woonsocket during the mid-nineteenth century. Many of their descendants are still there today, and they often speak to one another in their ancestors' native French language.

Residents gather at a Wampanoag powwow in Pawtucket.

became a magnet, attracting a steady stream of people from a wide variety of backgrounds and nationalities.

The first major wave of immigration happened during the 1820s when Irish Catholics from Ireland entered Rhode Island to escape their homeland's difficult economic conditions. The second wave occurred during the early- to mid-1860s when people from French-speaking Canada as well as Germany, Sweden, Portugal, and the Cape Verde Islands off the western coast of Africa made their way into the state.

Many of the Portuguese immigrants from Portugal and the Cape Verde Islands (a group of islands off the western coast of Africa) were very good at sailing ships on the sea. When they arrived in Newport and Providence during the 1860s, they found plenty of work on Rhode Island's many whaling

A young girl works with her mother at their family's store in Cranston.

ships. Descendants of these hard workers can still be found today in Providence's Fox Point community and in other places in the state.

In the 1890s many people from Italy, Greece, Russia, Poland, Syria, Lithuania, Armenia, Lebanon, and the Ukraine arrived. The last major wave of immigration took place in the 1950s as Hispanics from the Caribbean region and refugees from Southeast Asia looked for better opportunities.

Throughout the years, residents from other states around the country have made Rhode Island their home. No matter where they are from, residents of Rhode Island bring lively culture, religions, and traditions to help make the state a great place to live.

Italians made up the largest of the ethnic groups seeking opportunities in Rhode Island in the 1890s. Their deep-rooted heritage is very much alive today in Providence's Little Italy on Federal Hill—a bustling district with plenty of Italian restaurants, espresso shops, and bakeries.

Today's Population

According to data gathered from the 2000 U.S. Census, when it comes to racial and ethnic makeup, most Rhode Islanders are white, totaling 85 percent of the state's population. People of Hispanic or Latino heritage make up 8.7 percent, while African-Americans comprise 4.5 percent. The state's Asian population is 2.3 percent.

Before European settlement, the region's population was mostly Native Americans. Today, however, Native Americans number only about 5,000. More than half belong to the Narragansett group.

The Narragansett—like other Native American groups in the state—have not had an easy time. In the past, many opportunities offered to immigrants and people with other ethnic backgrounds were not available to the Narragansett. It was very difficult for many of them to succeed financially, while holding on to their traditional values and ways. To help change that, Native American leaders have been working with state officials on an economic plan that would help many Native Americans by creating more jobs. On the drawing board are plans for a gaming and entertainment center, a Native American museum, a library and research center, a cable television station, a trading post, forestry projects, commercial powwows, and other businesses.

Narragansett children at the Nuweetoon School in Exeter.

Recipe for Johnny Cakes

Johnny cakes are similar to pancakes, but they are made out of cornmeal instead of wheat flour. Rhode Island's early settlers learned to make them from the area's Native Americans. Johnny cakes were meant to be eaten hot, but were often cooled and then brought along on trips. For that reason they were called "journey cakes." Over the years the pronunciation of "journey cakes" has turned into "johnny cakes."

Ingredients:

1 cup of cornmeal
1 teaspoon of sugar
1/2 teaspoon of salt
1- 1/4 cups of boiling water
Shortening or butter

Combine the cornmeal, sugar, and salt in a bowl. Have an adult help you with the stove. Boil the water. Let the water cool a bit and the pour it over the mixture. The mixture should not be thick and not too watery.

Put a little shortening or butter on a pancake griddle or frying pan and heat the pan until the butter or shortening is melted. Once that is done, take a tablespoon, dip it into the batter, and drop a few spoonfuls of the mixture onto the pan. Fry the batter over medium heat for six minutes before turning it over with a spatula. Cook that side for an additional six minutes. The cakes should be a golden-brown color. When they are done, you can eat them plain or top them with honey, maple syrup, or powdered sugar.

The majority of Rhode Islanders—regardless of race or ethnic identity—seem to favor the state's cities over the rural areas. In fact 90 percent of them live in cities in the eastern section of the state. Eight of the cities in that region—Cranston, Central Falls, Providence, East Providence, Newport, Pawtucket, Warwick, and Woonsocket—have already been singled out as some of the most densely populated cities in the entire United States. The remaining 10 percent of Rhode Islanders are spread out among the small, outlying rural communities, farmlands, and islands.

An aerial view of the bustling city of Newport.

Although the differences in lifestyle between Rhode Island's urban and rural communities can be huge on the surface, the state's small size makes it really easy to move from one to the other. "I've been living in a very small, rural community for a few years now," remarks Little Compton resident Lisa Rigby. "However, I can hop in my car at any time and drive into a big city

Many families move to Rhode Island for the good school systems.

like Providence and go to an art show, a concert, or a museum in less than 45 minutes. That's what's great about living in a state like Rhode Island. No matter where you're situated, you never feel alone or isolated. Plus there's a variety of things to do, no matter what your lifestyle is."

Many residents find themselves driving to different parts of Rhode Island for a number of reasons. Many work in different towns from where

Many people come to Rhode Island for the universities and colleges. Rhode Island has many fine institutions. From Providence College to Rhode Island School of Design to Brown University, people from around the country—and around the world—move to Rhode Island to attend or work at the schools.

they live. Others like to visit many of Rhode Island's shopping malls or stores. The coastal regions are a favorite place for people who like to swim, sail, or fish. Rhode Islanders know that their state has a lot to offer.

Famous Rhode Islanders

George M. Cohan:
Composer, Actor, and Playwright

Thanks to George M. Cohan, musical comedy became a popular form of entertainment in America during the 1920s and 1930s. This Providence-born artist was the first songwriter to be awarded the Congressional Medal of Honor. He received it for composing the popular, troop-rallying World War I song "Over There." Other well-known Cohan-penned classics include "Yankee Doodle Dandy," "You're a Grand Old Flag," and "Give My Regards to Broadway."

Gilbert Stuart: Portrait Artist

Stuart was born in Saunderstown in 1755. Gilbert Stuart is known around the world for the portraits he painted of the presidents of the United States. In fact, you are probably quite familiar with one of his three portraits of George Washington, since it is the one that is featured on the one-dollar bill. It is estimated that Stuart painted over a thousand portraits throughout his life.

Nap Lajoie: Baseball Player

Napoleon Lajoie was born in Woonsocket in 1874. He played for the Philadelphia Phillies, the Philadelphia A's, and the Cleveland Indians. In 1901 he had the highest season batting average in American League history with an astounding .422. In 1937 he was elected to the Baseball Hall of Fame. Lajoie died in 1959.

Ida Lewis: Lighthouse Keeper

Ida Lewis was born in 1842 in Newport. Lewis had the important responsibility of maintaining Lime Rock Light Station. Besides making sure the lighthouse remained lit at night, lighthouse keepers were also expected to help rescue people who were drowning or had just been in a shipwreck. At one point, Lewis was known as "The Bravest Woman in America" and saved many lives. Many people respected her skills and bravery and the fact that she was a woman doing a job that usually went to men.

Sarah Whitman: Poet

Sarah Whitman was born in Providence in 1803. She was a published poet and also wrote essays about topics like spiritualism and literary criticism. Whitman was also an activist for many social issues, such as women's right to vote and access to equal education. She is also known for her relationship to the famous poet Edgar Allen Poe. Whitman died in 1878.

Kady Brownell: Civil War Soldier

Kady Brownell was born in Africa, but came to the United States in the 1800s. In the early 1860s, when her husband signed up to join the Rhode Island Infantry (a military unit), she joined as well. She traveled with her husband's infantry, became a fine sharpshooter, and learned to use a soldier's sword. As the troops marched into battle during the Civil War, Brownell carried the flag—an important responsibility that helped keep troops organized during battle. She also helped tend to wounded soldiers and was often referred to as a "Daughter of the Regiment."

Calendar of Events

Gaspee Days Colonial Encampment

Every June the city of Warwick celebrates the June 10, 1772 burning of the British customs vessel the *Gaspee* with a number of events. One of them is an historic encampment in which visitors get a feel for military life during Rhode Island's colonial period. Dozens of people camp out for the weekend event in authentic Revolutionary War-era gear.

Bristol Fourth of July Celebration

Established in 1785, this is the oldest continuous celebration of its kind in the United States. The event includes a parade, pageants, food, music, dancing, games, displays, and fireworks.

Black Ships Festival

This July event in Newport honors the establishment of relations between the United States and Japan in 1853 thanks to the efforts of Commodore Matthew Calbraith Perry, who was born in South Kensington, Rhode Island. Among the many activities are a samurai sword exhibit, Japanese art displays, all kinds of tasty Japanese food, and some martial arts demonstrations.

Washington County Fair

Held in rural Richmond, this mid-August event is Rhode Island's largest state fair. Among the many attractions are crafts, New England food, an amusement park, and performances by country music artists.

A parade

International Quahog Festival

If you like eating clams, you will probably love this August festival which pays tribute to the quahog. In addition to quahog chowder, you can try quahog cakes, quahog stuffies, quahog chili, fried quahogs, and quahogs on the half shell.

Scituate Art Festival

This well-established Columbus Day weekend event in the picturesque town of Scituate draws close to 300 exhibitors specializing in painting, sculpture, antiques, and crafts. The colorful fall foliage that appears in the surrounding area is also worth checking out.

Autumnfest

The northern city of Woonsocket plays host to this huge October event, which features food concessions, a gigantic midway, arts and crafts, a kiddie fest, and all kinds of musical entertainment.

Heritage Day Powwow

Held in Warwick, this November event presents a wonderful opportunity to learn about Rhode Island's remarkable Native American heritage. In addition to Native American singing and dancing, there are arts, crafts, and storytelling.

The waterfront festival

4 How It Works

Although Rhode Island is divided into five counties—Providence, Kent, Washington, Bristol, and Newport—there is no county government. The main units of local government within the state are its thirty-nine municipalities, which are made up of eight cities and thirty-one towns. The majority of these municipalities are presided over by a mayor and a city or town council.

As in other states, many of the towns in Rhode Island hold annual town meetings. These meetings originated during the colonial era, and all eligible voters can attend. While at these sessions, voters can approve local spending, pass laws, and even elect local officials.

Rhode Island's present state constitution was adopted in 1843 as a reaction to the Dorr Rebellion. Since then it has been amended—or changed — more than forty times. The constitution can be changed by a majority vote of the state's General Assembly, but it must be followed by a majority vote of the people.

This statue of Roger Williams is located in Providence.

Branches of Government

Executive The governor is head of the executive branch. He or she enforces the laws that the legislative branch passes. The executive branch also consists of a lieutenant governor, attorney general, secretary of state, and general treasurer. Each member of the executive branch gets into office through a popular election, and each serves a four-year term.

Legislative Rhode Island's legislative branch is called the General Assembly. It is made up of a fifty-member senate and a one hundred-member house of representatives. Members of both houses earn their jobs through popular elections, and each serves a two-year term. Rhode Island's General Assembly is responsible for making the state's laws and appointing justices to the state's supreme court.

Judicial Rhode Island's judicial branch interprets and applies the state's laws. The highest court is the supreme court. It is made up of a chief justice and four associate judges. The General Assembly chooses all five members, and each serves a life term. The state's main trial court is the superior court. It consists of nineteen judges whom the governor chooses with the Senate's approval. They also serve for life. In addition, Rhode Island has family, district, municipal, and probate courts. The governor, with the consent of the General Assembly, appoints these justices for life terms, too.

On a statewide level, a governor who is elected to a four-year term heads Rhode Island. Rhode Island has a legislative branch called the General Assembly. It is made up of senators and representatives. These officials represent specific regions of the state. The state also has representatives at the national level. Eligible voters elect two senators to serve six-year terms in Washington, D.C., and two members of the house of representatives to serve two-year terms.

How a Bill Becomes Law

State laws often start out as ideas from concerned residents. Any Rhode Islander can talk to their state legislators about issues that affect the state and its residents. If a resident—or a group of residents—has a suggestion for a new law, it can be presented to a state legislator. Often, the legislator will develop the idea into a bill. The bill is then presented to the legislator's division of the General Assembly. For example, if the legislator is a senator, the bill will be brought to the senate. If the legislator is a state representative, the bill is brought to the house of representatives.

The bill is given a specific number to identify it. It is then given to a committee to review. The committee members read and discuss the bill. If they like it, they can recommend that the bill gets passed as it is. They can also make changes, refer the bill to another committee, or recommend that the discussion of the bill should be postponed. The committee may also present the bill to their fellow legislators without saying whether or not they agree or disagree with it.

If the bill is recommended for passage it is discussed among the full senate or full house. Changes may be made or the bill might remain the same. If the legislators of one house approve the bill it is sent to the other house for approval. Once there, the bill follows the same process until it is approved.

A bill that has been approved by both houses is then sent to the governor. The governor can approve the bill by signing it, can allow it to pass without signing it, or he or she can veto, or reject, it. Even if a bill is vetoed, it still has a chance to be made into a law. If three-fifths of both houses vote again to approve the bill, they can override the governor's veto.

If there is something you feel strongly about in your community or your state, try contacting your local legislators. All of them are interested in hearing what Rhode Islanders have to say. Remember, you can make a difference.

To find contact information for Rhode Island's state legislators, visit this Web site:
http://www.sec.state.ri.us/elections/findyourofficials
You will need to know the name of your street, and the city or town you live in. If you are not sure, ask a parent, teacher, or librarian to help you.

The state capitol building in Providence. State legislators meet here to decide state laws.

5 Making a Living

Throughout the state's history, Rhode Islanders have found ways to survive on the land. From farming, ranching, fishing in the rivers, bays, and ocean, to eventually using the rivers to power mills, residents have managed to make a living. Over time, however, industries such as manufacturing, retail, service, and tourism have grown in importance.

Manufacturing

From the late 1700s to the early 1800s, Rhode Island businesspeople started using new ways to manufacture items. As a result, within less than 30 years, the small state had become a manufacturing giant. Its textile mills were thriving. Providence had also distinguished itself as the jewelry-making capital of North America.

During the entire nineteenth and early twentieth centuries, manufacturing was the most profitable industry in Rhode Island. In fact, more than half the state's entire workforce was employed in the state's various factories. Just before

Rhode Islands ports have almost always played an important role in the state's economy.

the beginning of World War I, however, manufacturing in the state began to steadily decline. The manufacturing industry boomed again during wartimes when supplies were needed, but it also had its highs and lows over the next several decades.

Today, manufacturing still plays an important role in the state's economy. Although only 22 percent of the state's current work force works in the manufacturing

In 1813 a Providence silversmith named Jabez Gorham started manufacturing silver spoons. The company he founded, Gorham Silverware Company, is still in business today and is the world's largest producer of sterling silver.

industry, the state's factories continue to make a variety of products that are in very high demand. When it comes to jewelry making in the United States, Rhode Island is still well respected. Rhode Island businesses still thrive on making jewelry and other items out of precious metals. Today there are hundreds of shops specializing in everything from silverware and silver-plated eating utensils and serving dishes to costume and fine jewelry.

Rhode Island continues to play a huge role in making fabricated metal products such as nuts, bolts, wires, tools, pipe fittings, and metal parts for machines. Other manufactured products that Rhode Islanders specialize in are toys, chemicals, plastics, textiles, transportation

A factory worker works on copper tubing.

An aerial view of Rhode Island farmland.

equipment, electronic equipment, and scientific equipment—particularly medical and surgical products.

Agriculture and Fishing

A little over 1 percent of Rhode Island's labor force is involved in agriculture, forestry, and fisheries. The state presently has about 700 farms, which are located primarily in the central parts of the state.

Some of Rhode Island's top agricultural products are nursery plants. These plants are grown in Rhode Island and then sent to different parts of the state or different states to be sold in nurseries. These include flowering plants, Christmas trees, sod, and decorative trees and shrubs. Some of Rhode

Island's farms have become well known for their potatoes, sweet corn, tomatoes, squash, cabbage, and snap beans.

Rhode Island also has a number of orchards that grow fruits such as peaches, pears, apples, and berries. In addition, a number of commercial vineyards have been established in Little Compton, Cumberland, Prudence Island, and South Kingstown. These vineyards grow grapes which are made into wine that is sold in Rhode Island or sent to other places.

Rhode Islanders farms and ranches also raise different types of livestock. These include dairy cows, hogs, and hens. The products that come from the livestock is often processed or prepared in the state and then shipped around the country.

In the seafood industry, Rhode Island is still an important contributor. Commerical fishing boats—boats that catch a very large amount of fish or other seafood to be sold—bring in a high number of flounder, cod, tuna, squid, scallops, and whiting. Rhode Island fishermen also harvest quahogs and lobsters.

Unfortunately, Rhode Island's seafood industry is presently threatened by the environmental decline of Narragansett Bay, where much of the state's fishing activities take place. This decline involves the pollution of the once-clean bay waters. State sewage treatment plants that were built in the 1800s are no longer effective. As a result, after a heavy rainfall, water tends to fill up the treatment plants, causing an overflow of sewage into the bay. This sewage is harming the fish and other sea creatures that make their homes in the bay. This, in turn, hurts the state's fishing industry. But by working together with concerned residents and businesspeople, environmental action groups such as the Save the Bay organization are fighting hard to correct the situation. Whether it is establishing new rules about the amount of sewage that can be processed or stored, or finding ways to fix the plants, everyone is looking hard for a solution.

Mining is not a huge industry in Rhode Island, but sand and gravel products have continued to play an important role in the state's ongoing highway reconstruction efforts.

Trap fishing along the coast is a popular way for Rhode Island fishermen to catch seafood.

Products & Resources

Metal Products

Rhode Island is well known for the jewelry, silverware, and other goods made out of precious metals like silver. Many stores and factories in the state still create these goods. The metal industry in Rhode Island also includes factories and plants that produce metal products for construction, tools, and other important objects.

Agricultural Products

Rhode Island yields a variety of agricultural products, ranging from flowering plants, decorative trees, and shrubs, to fruits and vegetable such as beans, tomatoes, pumpkins, potatoes, berries, apples, and corn. Different farms in Rhode Island also produce hay.

Toys

One of the world's leading toy manufacturers, Hasbro, got its start in the Ocean State. In 1923 brothers Henry and Helal Hassenfeld first started the company in Providence, selling items such as textiles and school supplies. Over the years the company eventually branched out to become a top name in toys. The company's main headquarters are currently in Pawtucket.

Seafood

Commercial fishing boats go into Rhode Island's coastal waters to catch a wide range of fish. They also harvest shellfish and other sea animals. Many Rhode Islanders also work in the factories and plants that clean, process, and pack these seafood products. The products are often shipped out to markets around the country and throughout the world.

Tourism

For a small state, Rhode Island has many things that attract millions of tourists every year. For those who like summer activities such as swimming, boating, and fishing, the state's numerous sandy beaches and ocean-side resorts are especially attractive. Rhode Island's rich history also draws people to the state. Many travel to the state to enjoy its historical sites and museums.

Scientific Instruments

Rhode Island manufacturers supply the health industry with many of the tools it needs to help people. Doctors and health-care workers around the country use Rhode Island-manufactured items such as syringes (needles used to draw blood), devices that measure blood pressure, and other important tools.

Service Industries

To make up for the decline of manufacturing and to help give Rhode Island's economy the boost it needed, state officials began attracting service industries into the region beginning in the early 1970s. People who work in service industries provide a service instead of make a product. Examples of service workers include salespeople, museum guides, teachers, bank tellers, nurses, and doctors. Over the years, the state's strong effort to attract service industries has certainly paid off. According to data gathered from the 2000 U.S. Census, those employed in Rhode Island's service industries account for 44 percent of the state's entire workforce.

The Arcade Mall in Providence has long been a popular place for residents and tourists.

Close to one-fourth of the 44 percent are employed in the area of health services. That includes doctors' offices, private hospitals, and various walk-in clinics. The next-largest group of service workers is made up of those who perform educational services, such as teachers and school administrators. People involved in finance, insurance, and real estate services also make up a sizeable portion of the service industry. Cities such as

Providence and Warwick host the headquarters for some large banks and financial institutions.

Tourism is Rhode Island's second-largest industry. It presently supports approximately more than 39,000 jobs. Tourists come to the state to enjoy its sites and activities. And fortunately for the state, when they come to Rhode Island they spend money. In 2000, the state produced more than $3.26 billion in tourism-related sales. The

Many leisure- and entertainment-related activities had their origins in historic Newport. In 1774 the town hosted the first circus in the country, as well as the first auto race in 1895. The first polo match in the United States was also played in Newport in 1876. The coastal town continues to attract many visitors every year.

Young visitors learn to tie nautical knots.

Making a Living

numbers of new jobs and sales dollars are expected to increase as Rhode Island's tourism industry grows.

Rhode Island certainly has plenty to offer. There are dozens of sandy beaches, a variety of boating and fishing opportunities, and plenty of historical sites. But most importantly, Rhode Island is full of hard working people who cherish their freedoms, their families, and their land. Perhaps that is why for almost four hundred years, Rhode Island has distinguished itself as a very attractive place to be.

A pair of Rhode Islanders enjoys the state's natural beauty.

Rhode Island

Rhode Island's state flag shows a golden anchor on a white background. Thirteen golden stars encircle the anchor. These stars represent the original thirteen colonies. Underneath the anchor is a blue ribbon with the word HOPE written in gold. This version of the flag was adopted in 1897.

The state seal depicts a golden anchor with the word HOPE above it. Written along the circular border of the seal are the words SEAL OF THE STATE OF RHODE ISLAND AND PROVIDENCE PLANTATIONS 1636. "1636" represents the year Roger Williams first established Rhode Island's first permanent European settlement. The seal was adopted in 1664.

RHODE ISLAND

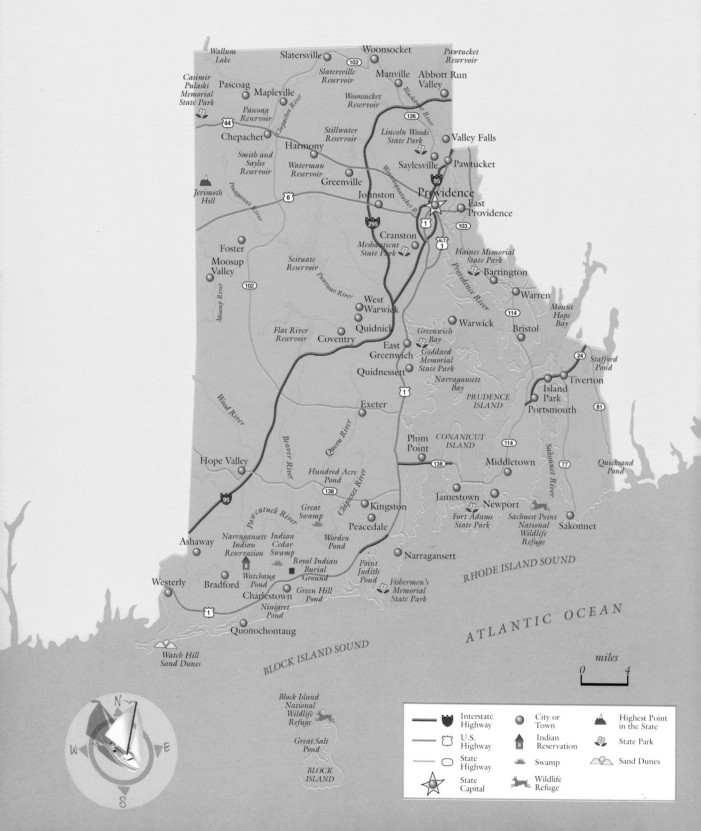

Wallum Lake
Slatersville
Woonsocket
Pawtucket Reservoir

Casimir Pulaski Memorial State Park
Pascoag
Mapleville
Slatersville Reservoir
102
Manville
Abbott Run Valley

Pascoag Reservoir
Woonsocket Reservoir
126
Blackstone River

44
Chepachet
Chepachet River
Stillwater Reservoir
Lincoln Woods State Park
Valley Falls

Harmony
Smith and Sayles Reservoir
Waterman Reservoir
Saylesville
Pawtucket

Jerimoth Hill
Ponaganset River
6
Greenville
Johnston
95
Providence
East Providence

Woonasquatucket R.
1
103

Foster
Meshanticut State Park
Cranston
ALT 1

Moosup Valley
Scituate Reservoir
295
Haines Memorial State Park
Barrington

102
Moosup River
Pawtuxet River
West Warwick
Warren
114

Flat River Reservoir
Quidnick
Coventry
Greenwich Bay
Warwick
Providence River
Mount Hope Bay

East Greenwich
Goddard Memorial State Park
Bristol

Wood River
Quidnessett
Narragansett Bay
24
Stafford Pond
Tiverton

1
Island Park
Portsmouth
81

Exeter
Beaver River
Queen River
PRUDENCE ISLAND

Plum Point
CONANICUT ISLAND
114
Sakonnet River

Hope Valley
Hundred Acre Pond
Chipuxet River
138
Middletown
77
Quicksand Pond

95
Pawcatuck River
Great Swamp
Kingston
Jamestown
Newport

Peacedale
Fort Adams State Park
Sachuest Point National Wildlife Refuge
Sakonnet

Ashaway
Narragansett Indian Reservation
Indian Cedar Swamp
Worden Pond
Point Judith Pond
Narragansett

Westerly
Bradford
Watchaug Pond
Royal Indian Burial Ground
Green Hill Pond
Fishermen's Memorial State Park
RHODE ISLAND SOUND

Charlestown
Ninigret Pond
Quonochontaug

Watch Hill Sand Dunes
BLOCK ISLAND SOUND
ATLANTIC OCEAN

miles
0   4

N
W   E
S

Block Island National Wildlife Refuge
Great Salt Pond
BLOCK ISLAND

Legend

- **Interstate Highway**
- **U.S. Highway**
- **State Highway**
- **State Capital**
- **City or Town**
- **Indian Reservation**
- **Swamp**
- **Wildlife Refuge**
- **Highest Point in the State**
- **State Park**
- **Sand Dunes**

Rhode Island

Words and music by Thomas Clarke Brown

MORE ABOUT RHODE ISLAND

Books

Brennan, Linda Crotta. *The Black Regiment of the American Revolution.* North Kingstown, R.I.: Moon Mountain Publishing, 2004.

Doak, Robin S. *Rhode Island.* New York: Children's Press, 2004.

Mattern, Joanne. *Rhode Island, the Ocean State.* Milwaukee, WI: World Almanac Library, 2003.

Web sites

Official Site of the State of Rhode Island:
http://www.ri.gov/index.php

Rhode Island History
http://www.rilin.state.ri.us/studteaguide/RhodeIslandHistory/rodehist.html

Visit Rhode Island—Rhode Island Tourism Division
http://www.visitrhodeisland.com

About the Author

Rick Petreycik is a writer whose articles on history, music, film, and business have appeared in *American Legacy, Rolling Stone, Yankee, Disney Magazine,* and *The Hartford Courant,* among other publications. He lives in Connecticut with his wife, Pattilee, and daughter, Caitlin.

Index

Page numbers in **boldface** are illustrations.

maps,
  Rhode Island, **6, 76**
  United States, **1**

AfricanAmericans, 35, 49
agriculture, 14, 67-68, **67**, 70,
  70
Algonquian, 23
animals, 4, **4**, 5, **5**, 17-21, **17,
  18, 19, 21**
Aquidneck Island, 12
Asians, 49
Atlantic Ocean, 7, 10, **10**

Battle of Rhode Island, 35
bays, 7, 11, 12, 13
beach, 10, **10, 74**
Belmonts, 41
birds, 4, **4**, 20, 21, **21**
Block,
  Adriaen, 25, **25**
  Island, 11, **11**, 12, 25
bowenite, 5, **5**
Brown,
  John, 34
  Moses, 36
Brownell, Kady, 55, **55**

Canonicus, 28
capital, 14, **58**, 63, **63**
  See also Providence
Civil War, 39-41, **40**, 55
climate, 15-16
coast, 7, 10-14, **10, 12**, 17, 31
Cohan, George M., 54, **54**
colony, 26, 28
counties, 59
craft activity, 32-33, **32-33**
Cranston, 14, 52
crops, 14, 23, 31, 67, 68, 70,
  70
cumberlandite, 5, **5**

Dodge, Nehemiah, 38
Dorr,
  Rebellion, 38-39
  Thomas, 38-39

Dudington, William, 35

economy, 65-74
England *See* Great Britain

factories, 41, 42, **42**, 43
farms, 14, 23, 31, 37, 47, 65,
  67-68, **67**, 70
festivals, 56-57, **56-57**
fish, 17, 19, **19, 64** 65, 68,
  69, **69**
flooding, 16
flowers, 4, **4**, 17, 19, **19**
forests, 13, 14, **14**, 16, 23
France, 34, 35

Gaspee, 34, **34**
glaciers, 8
government, 59-63
Gorham, Jabez, 66
Great Britain, 34, 35-36
Great Depression, 43
Great Swamp Fight, 29

Hasbro, 70
Hassenfeld, Henry and Helal,
  70
highest point, 14
Hispanic, 48, 59
history, 22-45
hurricanes, 15

immigration, 37, 41, 47-49
islands, 12, 31

Jerimoth Hill, 14
jewelry, 38, 41, 66, 70, **70**

King Philip's War, 29-31
Kingston, 29

Lajoie, Nap, 54, **54**
lakes, 8, 9, **9**, 17
lawmaking, 60, 61-62
Lewis, Ida, 55, **55**
lighthouse, 11, **11**, 55
livestock, 68

manufacturing, 35, 36, 37, 38,
  43, 44, 47, 65, 66, **66**, 70,
  70, 71, **71**
Massachusetts Bay Colony, 26,
  29
Massasoit, 28
Metacomet, 29
Miantonomo, 28
militia, 35
mills, 36, 38, 40, 65
minerals, 5, **5**
Mohegan, 29, 30
molasses, 31
Morgans, 41

name, 25
Narragansett
  Bay, 5, 7, 8, **8**, 12, 15, 26,
    34, **34**
  Native people, 23, 25, 28,
    50, **50**
Native Americans, 5, 19, 23-
  25, **23**, 26, **27**, 28, 29-31
  , **30, 46**, 47, 49, 50, **50**
Newport, 12, **12**,13, 28, 31,
  35, 41, 48, 52, **52**
Niantic, 23
nickname, 4
Nipmuc, 23, 30

Pawtucket, 37, **37**, 52, 70
Pawtuxet River, 9, 36
Pequot, 23
Podunk, 30
pollution, 68-69
population, 4, 37, 49
Portsmouth, 28
Providence
  city of, 13, **13**, 31, 34, 36,
    38, 39, **39**, 44, **44**,
    48, 52, 63, **63**, 70
  River, 12, 16
Puritans, 26

quahog, 5, **5**

railroad, 37

ranching, 65
recipe, 51, **51**
Revolutionary War, 35-36
rivers, 8, 14, 17, 36, 37

schools, 50, **50,** 53, **53**
Scituate Reservoir, 9
sea trade, 31, 34, 37
seafood, **64,** 65, 68-69, **69,**
    71, **71**
service, 72-74
settlers, 25, 28, 29, 30, **30,** 31
Slater, Samuel, 36-37
slavery, 31, 39, 40
sounds, 7,
Stamp Act, 34
state
    borders, 7
    flag, 75, **75**
    seal, 75, **75**
    size, 7
    song, 77
    symbols, 4-5, **4-5**
statehood, 4, 36
Stuart, Gilbert, 54, **54**
sugar, 31
    Act, 34

textiles, 36, 40, 43, 65
time line, 45
tourism, 71, **71,** 72-74
toys, 70, **70**
trees, 4, **4,** 14, **14,** 15, 16, **16,**
    19,
Triangular Trade, 31

Vanderbilts, 41
Verrazzano, Giovanni da, 25

Wampanoag, 23, **23,** 25, 28
Warwick, 14, 28, 52
Web sites, 62, 78
West Indies, 31
whaling, 31, 37
Whitman, Sarah, 55, **55**
wildlife, 4, **4,** 5, **5,** 16-21, **16,**
    17, 18, 19, 21
    endangered, 20-21
Wilkinson, David, 37

Williams, Roger, 26, **27,** 28,
    29, 58, **58**
Woonsocket, 14, 47, 52
World War I, 42
World War II, 43